CREEPY Cute

crochet

CREEPY Cute
crochet

Zombies, Ninjas, Robots, and More!

By Christen Haden

QUIRK BOOKS

PHILADELPHIA

Library of Congress Cataloging in Publication Number: 2007943161
ISBN: 978-1-59474-232-3
Printed in China

Typeset in Syntax, MonsterFonts, and Wendy LP
Designed by Karen Onorato
Photography by Chad VanPelt

Distributed in North America by Chronicle Books
680 Second Street
San Francisco, CA 94107

10 9 8 7 6 5 4 3

Quirk Books
215 Church Street
Philadelphia, PA 19106
www.quirkbooks.com

WHAT LURKS WITHIN . . .

BECOMING DR. FRANKENSTEIN
WITH A CROCHET HOOK AND YARN
(or, Why I Created the Creatures in This Book)

It all started with zombies.

I have a bit of a soft spot for zombie flicks. Old-school shamblers, recent remake runners, undead animated by magic or mad science—you name it, I'm there with popcorn.

So, it seemed a no-brainer when zombies started popping up in my work as well. After all, I tend to make things that I like.

Of course, the royal We tries not to be a one-trick pony. The original zombie needed companions. Skeletons. Ghosts. Vampires.

These, in turn, required worthy adversaries in the form of knights and ancient warriors.

. . . and, after that, I needed monkeys. Because monkeys are cool.

Now, at this point I could have kept the arcane secrets of this ragtag horde to myself. However, every evil genius knows that her creations are best when unleashed on the more general public. This is where you, the reader, come in.

This army of creatures needs to grow, and my ability to add new members is finite. With the patterns included in this book, you should be able to make an eclectic legion of cuteness for your very own—a force suitable for defending (or conquering) cubicles, bookshelves, desktops . . . really, any sort of environment vulnerable to the fiber arts.

So, go forth and create. Craft, my minions!

A FEW THINGS TO KNOW BEFORE YOU BEGIN

This book contains all you need to know to crochet up your very own horde of creepy cute creatures. It offers easy-to-follow instructions and patterns for beginners through master crafters. Those who have never before touched a crochet hook and yarn may find it useful to consult a true "learn to crochet" step-by-step instruction book to master the basics. You can teach yourself to crochet, often in as little as one day (it's true!). After that, you're set to craft these adorable one-of-a-kind dolls.

Resources

All the materials you need are as close as your local craft store. But it's always fun to experiment and explore the wide world of yarns and notions. You may find the following suppliers useful in your crafting adventures.

Lion Brand Yarn • www.lionbrand.com
My choice for the projects in this book.

Yarndex • www.yarndex.com
Yarn directory with profiles of more than 3,000 yarns.

Craft Yarn Council of America • www.craftyarncouncil.com
The site for free projects, online help, and all things knitting and crochet related.

Bernat • www.bernat.com
Books, yarns, free patterns galore.

Coats & Clark • www.coatsandclark.com
For all your needle-crafting needs.

Hello Yarn • www.helloyarn.com
High-quality hand-painted and handspun yarns, for the crafty connoisseur.

Charm Woven Labels • www.charmwoven.com
Distinctive personalized labels for all your crochet projects.

And, of course, we find an endless source of inspiration in other people's handmade wonders, so be sure to check out the crafting community on Etsy.com.

TOOLS OF THE TRADE

Unlike the complicated laboratory in which Dr. Frankenstein constructed his scary monster, crocheting these delightfully creepy dolls requires only a few common crafty items.

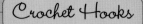

Crochet Hooks

You'll probably need only one hook (maybe two) to make everything in this book. I suggest a U.S. size E (3.5 mm), which will work well for most of the main body parts. A U.S. size 1 (2.75 mm) hook may come in handy for chain-stitch edgings and details such as hair. Experiment with hook sizes to achieve a gauge of 10 sc x 10 rows = about 2" x 2". If you plan to crochet for long periods or are prone to hand trouble, Clover Soft Touch hooks are most comfortable.

Yarn

I provide color suggestions in each pattern, but don't let that stop you from doing your own thing! Any worsted-weight yarn will work well, but if you want your creature to look exactly like the one pictured, use Lion Brand Cotton-Ease yarn since that's what I chose for all the examples in this book.

Yarn labels identify yarn weight, which is usually printed as a number. (See the Craft Yarn Council Web site for more information.) All the projects in this book call for a medium yarn weight of **4** (as on the icon, left). Your yarn choices include **acrylic** (cheap and easy to find); **cotton** (also easy to find and cheap but yields crisp, defined stitches); and **wool** (try different types; the finished look of items made with wool yarn varies widely).

If you can't find just the right color or have yarn that's too thin, try plying together different yarns and threads. DMC embroidery floss, pearl cotton, and crochet thread come in a wide array of colors and can be easily mixed in with fingering or lace-weight yarns. Generally, plying together two or three strands of yarn and thread will yield about the same gauge as one ply of worsted-weight yarn.

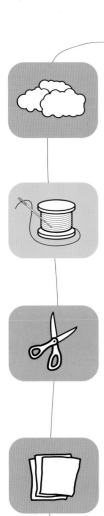

Stuffing

Your stuffing options are polyester fiberfill or poly-pellets. I usually combine the two, filling the bottom of the body with pellets and the rest with fiberfill to help with stability.

Needle and Thread

Just about any basic sewing needle will suit, as long as it's reasonably sharp and not too big. If you're attaching beads or handmade polymer clay buttons, beading needles (or really thin needles) are useful but not necessary.

Scissors

Just about any functional pair of scissors will do, though small embroidery scissors are particularly good at cutting felt and snipping the ends of loose yarn. Pendant-type yarn cutters can also be helpful while crafting out and about.

Felt

You can certainly use the inexpensive synthetic felt that comes in individual squares, but if possible, spring for the better-quality brands that contain wool. Real wool (or wool-blend) felt is easier to work with. Small pieces are less likely to fall apart, and cut edges stay crisper.

These are the basic materials you need to make me and my friends!

Optional Materials

These items may come in handy but aren't necessary.

Felting needles are useful for attaching bits of yarn and felt without gluing or sewing. But be careful: They're sharp and thin, and it's easy to prick your finger or break off the end of one inside a doll.

Glue should be strong enough to keep pieces from pulling off easily and thick enough not to run while you work with it.

Bamboo skewer or toothpick is needed only if you choose to make eyes from polymer clay (rather than using buttons, notions, or found materials). I blunt my skewer slightly to make sure the hole is big enough to pull a needle through.

Polymer clay is also needed only if you choose to make the creatures' eyes yourself. I like Premo! Sculpey, though standard Sculpey will work, too. FIMO Classic is much firmer and generally needs to be worked a while so that it's not too crumbly.

X-acto knife is also needed primarily for making clay eyes. A standard #1 precision knife works well.

Jeepers creepers! My peepers are made from polymer clay.

HOOK 'EM UP: CROCHET BASICS

Crochet patterns use abbreviations for stitches and directions. This shorthand tells you what stitches to make when. Many of the directions also come with a chart that communicates visually what the directions say to do. The chart uses symbols for each stitch; for example, a chain stitch is an oval and a single crochet is a small "X." The boxes below give you all the abbreviations in this book as well as the corresponding symbol used in the patterns.

The patterns in this book also use **brackets [ ]** to indicate a group of stitches to be made all at once or to be repeated a certain number of times. **Parentheses ( )** are used within brackets to further set off stitches. **Curly brackets { }** at the end of a line indicate the number of stitches you should end up with.

Abbreviations	
ch	chain
dc	double crochet
dec	decrease
dtr	double triple crochet
hdc	half-double crochet
inc	increase
prev	previous
sc	single crochet
sl st(s)	slip stitch(es)
st(s)	stitch(es)
tr	triple crochet

Stitch Key			
		╱	slip stitch (sl st)
0	chain stitch (ch)	T	half double crochet (hdc)
X	single crochet (sc)	∓	double crochet (dc)
⩔	increase (inc)	∓	triple crochet (tr)
⩕	decrease (dec)	∓	double triple crochet (dtr)

A Note About Gauge

Gauge is important because it tells you how big (or small) to make your crochet craft. It indicates the number of stitches and rows per inch. Almost all the projects in this book have a gauge of 5 sc x 5 rows = 1" x 1", meaning that there will be 5 stitches and 5 rows per inch.

Special Techniques

Some of the patterns in this book call for techniques you may not find in standard crochet patterns. These are marked by a dagger (†) and are explained below.

Magic Ring

1. Make a loop with the stray end under the working end of the yarn.

2. With the hook, pull the working end from behind the stray end under and back up to the top. Ch 1 or otherwise start as you would any type of ring.

3. Continue around, working as usual with the sts worked directly over both cords.

4. Once you have worked the desired number of sts, hold work with one hand and pull the stray end taut with the other. Continue to pull the stray end until the ring is the desired size. Weave in the end to keep the ring from growing as piece is worked.

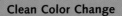

Clean Color Change

1. When a "clean color change sl st" is called for, work the round as usual until the last st. Before making a sl st to close the round, pull out the hook, put it back through the st where the sl st would go, and put the working loop behind the piece.

2. Make the sl st with the new color, pulling it through both loops.

3. Continue to work round as usual.

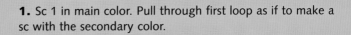

4. The result is a more regular color change.

Pattern Stitch

1. Sc 1 in main color. Pull through first loop as if to make a sc with the secondary color.

2. Pull through the second loop to finish the sc with the main color.

3. Repeat the above steps for the number of sts needed in pattern stitch.

1. Cut.

2. Pull loop through.

3. Thread end through first stitch of round.

4. Thread end back through last stitch of round.

See the pattern stitch in action on page 81.

EMBELLISHMENTS & WEAPONRY

Most of the dolls in the book have the same basic parts—head, body, arms—and you'll find directions for creating those on pages 94–95. But the devil is in the details, and the little touches are what give these dolls their cuddly (yet somewhat scary) charm. Below are some tips for creating unique creature features.

Hair

Many of the dolls are topped with sleek tresses formed of looped fringe (described below). But hair can be made using a variety of techniques and materials, so experiment with yarns, fabrics, or fibers to find that perfect set of locks for your vampire or zombie.

Fringe

To make fringe hair, you'll need yarn in the desired hair color with matching string, a crochet hook (U.S. size 1), and a hairpin lace tool (either a fork or loom). If you can't find this tool, use a piece of cardboard in the desired width, though it will be harder to slide off the finished fringe. The hairpin fork used in the examples is 2 1/4" wide. Substituting a wider fork will result in longer hair; a narrower one will yield shorter hair.

Creating Fringe

1. Start by working a ch 1 with the string. Holding the yarn in place with your working hand, wrap the yarn around the hairpin fork once, clockwise.

2. Holding the hook in front of the yarn, pull the string behind the piece just wrapped around.

3. Ch 1. Repeat steps 1 through 3 until you have enough fringe to cover the doll's head and then fasten off.

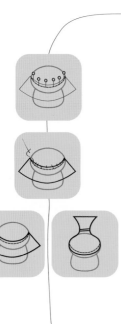

Attaching Fringe Hair

1. Pin the fringe along the hairline, with the chain edge sitting slightly behind the hairline and the fringe pointed in the opposite direction of how it will sit when finished.

2. Stitch along the fringe, next to the chain edge, making sure to catch both the fringe and the head.

3. Flip the fringe over the newly stitched seam. The hair will need to be held in place, either by tying it into a ponytail or tacking it in place with a felting needle or needle and thread.

Eyes

Your choice of eyes greatly affects the creature's overall character, so select a pair of peepers that suits its personality. Some possibilities are:

Buttons. *Pros:* Easy to find, simple to attach, and available in a slew of styles. *Cons:* You'll need tiny buttons for most of the dolls in this book. And remember: They are a choking hazard.

Beads. *Pros:* Generally inexpensive (especially if you're making a lot of dolls), easy to achieve consistent results. *Cons:* The selection might be limited, and, like buttons, they are a choking hazard.

Safety Eyes or Button Eyes. *Pros:* Easily yield professional-looking results. Safety eyes are, as the name implies, safe for children. *Cons:* You may have difficulty finding eyes small enough to suit the dolls in this book; limited selection.

Embroidery. *Pros:* Complete control over size/style/look. Limited choking hazard. *Cons:* Can require some skill and patience to achieve a nice, even appearance.

Polymer Clay. All the creatures in this book have eyes made from polymer clay. The clay package usually contains instructions for baking and hardening. Finished facial features should be no more than 1/16" thick. *Pros:* Control over the size/style/look. Very inexpensive (particularly if you're making a lot). *Cons:* Difficult to achieve consistent results from batch to batch. Can be time consuming, depending on your level of perfectionism. Possible choking hazard.

Here are directions for creating the two most common types of clay eyes:

Plain Eye. Roll a ball of clay no larger than 1/4" diameter (the smaller the better), press it into a disk, and place on a baking sheet. If you plan to sew the eyes onto the doll, before baking use a bamboo skewer or toothpick to poke two holes through the clay disk. If you plan to attach the eyes with glue, bake according to package directions. Done!

"Pie-Wedge" Eye. You'll need white, translucent, and black polymer clay. Flatten a small ball of translucent clay to about 1/4"–3/8" diameter and 1/8" thick. Make another ball using black clay, this time about 1/8"–1/4" in diameter and 1/8" thick. Using an X-acto knife, cut a small wedge from the black ball. Press it into the translucent round until you have a dish about 3/8"–1/2" diameter. If desired, press 2 tiny dots of white on top of the black part. Tah-dah!

My hair and eyes are what make me special!

17

Arms & Armaments

Sometimes a creature needs a weapon to pull the look together. Below are instructions for a few trimmings in felt or clay.

Axe, Mace, Sword

Necessary items for all Vikings, Trojans, Spartans, and such.

1. Cut 2 in felt from each template (below).

2. With black thread, stitch each weapon's design through one of its two cutouts, as shown.

3. Glue second cutout to the back of the first. Trim away excess felt along edges.

Spear

The spiky accoutrement of a mighty Amazon.

1. Flatten a piece of gray or silver clay, a little more than $1/16$" thick. Use an X-acto knife to cut out a spearhead according to template at left.

2. Flatten a piece of brown clay, about $2^{3}/4$" long. Press it onto the spearhead, with the top slightly overlapping the spearhead.

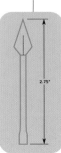

3. Roll a thin rope of beige clay, less than 1/16" thick. Cut three tiny pieces and wrap them over the join between the spearhead and the shaft. Press lightly in place.

For the Grim Reaper's harvest, of course.

1. Roll a piece of black clay into a tube about 2 1/2" long and 3/16" thick. Roll a piece of silver (or gray) clay into a tube about 3/4" long and 1/4" thick.

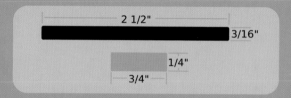

2. Taper the silver piece slightly on one end and flatten. Pull into a slight curve.

3. Carefully slit the top of the black tube in half and press the silver blade into the gap.

PUTTING IT ALL TOGETHER

Now comes the real fun—assembling your creepy cute creature. Making the dolls is as easy as 1-2-3.

1. Crochet each part of the doll. Most of the dolls are made up of a basic head, body, and arms. The patterns for these "basic parts" are on pages 94–95. Some have special appendages, like tentacles, tails, and top hats; the patterns for these are included with the instructions for each doll. Some creatures also look best with hair, so you'll want to make that, too. Instructions for creating fringed 'dos begin on page 15.

2. Stuff the body parts that need stuffing, usually the head, arms, and body. The instructions for each doll will tell you what additional parts need to be stuffed. For stuffing tips, see "The Insides," opposite.

3. Sew the parts together, as directed in the instructions.

You're done!

The diagrams that accompany the directions show you where to sew the pieces together, like this:

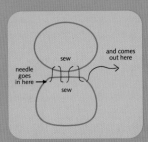

Easy! But watch out for sloppy stitching. Here are a few tips to prevent Lopsided Doll Syndrome:

• Take your time and pay attention to stitch placement.

• Try to catch a whole strand with the needle instead of splitting the yarn.

• When possible, match stitches (connect each individual stitch with one other individual stitch).

The Insides

Each creature is a bit smushy, thanks to their soft innards (see "Stuffing," page 9). There really aren't many stuffing techniques to share. You just put the stuff in. But here are a few finer points:

Understuffing/Overstuffing

Use enough stuffing so that the finished doll keeps its shape, but not so much that it starts to bulge or stuffing pops out between the stitches.

Lumpy Stuffing

It's actually pretty easy to unevenly stuff a doll. After stuffing, roll the piece in your palms to even out the form.

Balance

If your doll is top-heavy (or front- or side-heavy), it won't stand upright. To fix a wobbly doll, weight the base by pouring poly-pellets in first and then topping off with fiberfill.

Our insides are squishy but even. Otherwise, we can't stand up!

THE CREATURES

DEVIL

Apparently, he's in the details.

Difficulty Level: Intermediate • **Gauge:** 5 sc x 5 rows = 1" x 1"

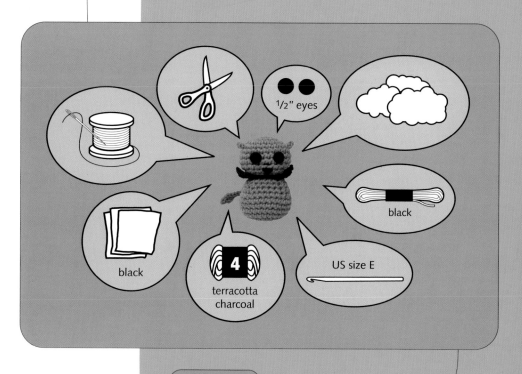

Basics

Body

Use terracotta-colored yarn and make 1 Basic Body (see pattern on page 94).

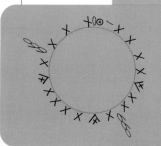

Head

Use terracotta-colored yarn and make 1 Basic Head (see pattern on page 95), but work row 4 as follows:

Row 4: Ch 1, sc 1 in same, sc 2, ch 3, sl st 2 in chain, sc 1, inc, sc 4, inc, sc 1, ch 3, sl st 2 in chain, sc 2, inc, sc 4, sl st to close round.

Details

Goatee

Cut a triangle of black felt, about $^3/_8$" long on each side.

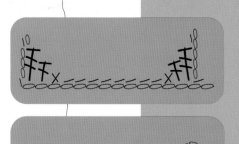

Collar

Use charcoal-colored yarn. Ch 15, sl st 2 from hook, ch 5, sl st 2 from hook, tr in same st as first sl st, dc 1, sc 1, sl st 8, sc 1, dc 1, tr 1, ch 1, sl st in front 2 loops of tr, ch 3, sl st in same st as tr. Fasten off.

Tail

Use terracotta-colored yarn. Ch 20, dc 3 sts from hook, ch 1, sl st in front 2 loops of dc, ch 2, sl st in same st as dc, sl st to end of chain. Fasten off.

Assembly

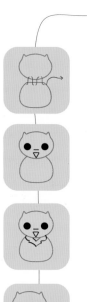

1. Stuff head and body and stitch together.

2. Using black embroidery floss, stitch mouth. Stitch or glue goatee below mouth. Attach eyes.

3. Wrap collar around neck. Stitch into place.

4. Tack tail onto back of body.

NOSFERATU

Bloodthirsty, yes.
But adorable too.

Difficulty Level: Intermediate • **Gauge:** 5 sc x 5 rows = 1" x 1"

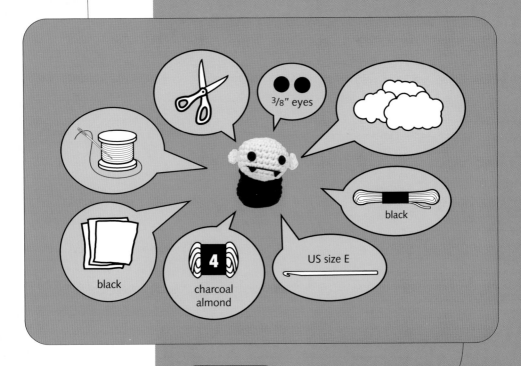

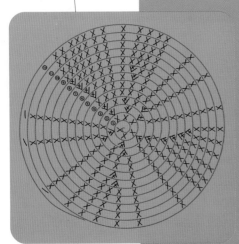

Basics

Head
Use almond-colored yarn and make 1 Basic Head (see pattern on page 95).

Body
Use charcoal-colored yarn.
Row 1: Sc 6 in magic ring† {6}.
Row 2: [Inc] around {12}.
Row 3: [Sc 1, inc] around {18}.
Row 4: Sc around {18}.
Row 5: [Sc 8, inc] twice {20}.
Row 6: [Sc 4, inc] around {24}.
Row 7: [Sc 5, inc] around {28}.
Row 8: [sc 13. inc] around {30}.
Row 9: Sc around {30}.
Row 10: Sc around {30}.
Row 11: Sc around {30}.
Row 12: Sc around, sl st, sl st {30}. Clean fasten off†.

† Stitches explained on pages 12 and 14.

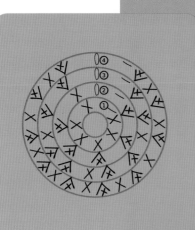

Body Base

Use charcoal-colored yarn.

Row 1: Sc 6 in magic ring†, sl st to close round {6}.

Row 2: Ch 1, sc 1 in same, [inc] around, sl st to close round {11}.

Row 3: Ch 1, inc, inc, [sc 1, inc, inc] around, sl st to close round {19}.

Row 4: Before working each stitch in this round, put the hook through the back loop of the next st on edge of top piece, joining the top and base. (Alternately, you may work the round normally and stitch together the top and base afterward.) Ch 1, inc, [sc 1, inc] around {29}. Clean fasten off†.

† Stitch explained on page 14.

Details

Collar

Use charcoal-colored yarn. Ch 25, sc 1, hdc 1, dc 1, ch 1, sl st in front two loops of dc, sl st, ch 1, tr 1, dc 13, tr 1, ch 1, sl st in main chain, ch 2, sl st in ch 2, dc 1, hdc 1, sc 1. Clean fasten off†.

Ears

Use almond-colored yarn.

Ear #1: Ch 2, sc 3 in first ch st, ch 2, sl st in ch 2, sl st in same st as prev sc. Fasten off.

Ear #2: Ch 4, sl st, sc 3 in first ch st, sl st in same. Fasten off.

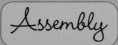

Assembly

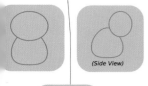

(Side View)

1. Stuff head and body and stitch head to front of body, as close to the top as possible. Nosferatu is a bit front-heavy because of the way his head is attached (see "side view"), so it helps to weight the bottom of his body with poly-pellets or hefty stuffing material.

2. Wrap collar around neck. Stitch into place.

3. Cut two 5" segments of charcoal-colored yarn. Knot each piece twice around the middle, with knots spaced about ¼" apart. Pull ends through the body and tack in place.

4. Using black embroidery floss, stitch mouth.

5. Cut black felt into two triangles measuring about ¼" on each side. Stitch or glue in place under mouth.

6. Stitch on ears.

7. Attach eyes.

QUEEN VAMPIRE

Be sure to keep her majesty out of the sun.

Difficulty Level: Intermediate • **Gauge:** 5 sc x 5 rows = 1" x 1"

 3/8" eyes

black

red
black

4

charcoal
almond

US size E

Basics

Head

Use almond-colored yarn and make 1 Basic Head (see pattern on page 95).

Body

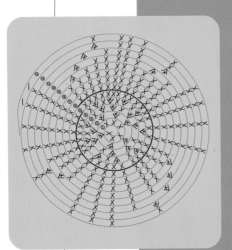

Use charcoal-colored yarn.
Row 1: Sc 6 in magic ring† {6}.
Row 2: [Inc] around {12}.
Row 3: [Inc, inc, sc 1] around {20}.
Row 4: [Inc, sc 1] around {30}.
Row 5: Sc around {30}.
Row 6: Sc around in back loops {30}.
Row 7: Sc around {30}.
Row 8: Sc around {30}.
Row 9: [Sc 13, dec] around {28}.
Row 10: [Sc 5, dec] around {24}.
Row 11: [Sc 4, dec] around {20}.
Row 12: [Sc 8, dec] around {18}.
Row 13: Sc around, sl st, sl st {18}. Clean fasten off†.

† Stitches explained on pages 12 and 14.

Join again in the front loops left from row 6. Work around as follows: Ch 2, dc 1, ch 1, sl st in front loops of prev dc, dc 2 in 1, ch 1, sl st in front loops of prev dc, [dc 2, ch 1, sl st in front loops of prev dc, dc 2 in 1, ch 1, sl st in front loops of prev dc] around. Fasten off.

Details

Collar

Use charcoal-colored yarn. Ch 18, sl st, ch 4, tr 1 in same st as first sl st, tr 16 ch 1, sl st in front 2 loops of prev tr, ch 3, sl st in same space as prev tr. Fasten off.

Assembly

1. Stuff head and body and stitch together.

2. Wrap collar around neck and pull tightly. Tie or stitch in place.

3. Create hair and stitch onto head (see "Hair," page 15).

4. Using black embroidery floss, stitch mouth. Cut black felt into two triangles measuring about 1/4" on each side. Stitch or glue in place under mouth.

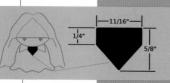

11/16"
1/4"
5/8"

5. Cut red felt according to template. Stitch or glue vest in place under collar.

6. Attach eyes.

CTHULHU

Crazy cute!

Difficulty Level: Intermediate • **Gauge:** 5 sc x 5 rows = 1" x 1"

³/₈" pie-wedge eyes

US size E

4 lime

Basics

Body and Arms
Use lime-colored yarn and make 1 Basic Body and 2 Basic Arms (see patterns on page 94).

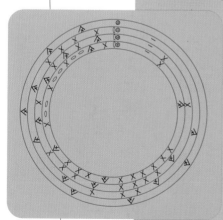

Tentacle Head
Use lime-colored yarn and begin Basic Head (see pattern on page 95). Work first 8 rows as directed and then work as follows:

Row 9: Ch 1, sc 1, dec, [ch 2, skip 1, sc 1] 3 times, dec, sc 3, dec, sc 6, dec, sc 1, sl st to close round.

Row 10: Ch 1, dec, [sc 1, dec] 3 times, sc 3, dec, sc 4, dec, sc 2, sl st to close round.

Row 11: Ch 1, sc 4, dec 3 times, sc 3, dec, dec, sl st to close round.

Row 12: Dec around to close. Fasten off; stitch up base.

For each gap formed by the [ch 2, skip 1] above:
Row 1: Join in the gap, ch 1, sc 5, sl st to close round {5}. Ch 1, sc 5, sl st to close round. Fasten off.

Details

Use lime-colored yarn.

Wing #1: Ch 6, sl st 3 sts from hook, tr 2 in 1st ch st, ch 2, sl st in front 2 loops of tr, tr 3 in 1st ch st. Fasten off.

Wing #2: Ch 4, tr 2 in 1st ch st, ch 2, sl st in front 2 loops of tr, tr 2 in 1st ch st, ch 2, sl st in front 2 loops of tr, ch 4, sl st in 1st ch. Fasten off.

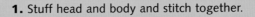

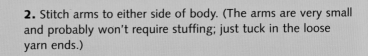

Assembly

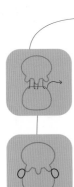

1. Stuff head and body and stitch together.

2. Stitch arms to either side of body. (The arms are very small and probably won't require stuffing; just tuck in the loose yarn ends.)

3. Stitch wings to back of body. The right side of each wing should face out.

4. Attach eyes.

36

SKELETON BRIDE & GROOM

Till death do them part.

Difficulty Level: Beginner • **Gauge:** 5 sc x 5 rows = 1" x 1"

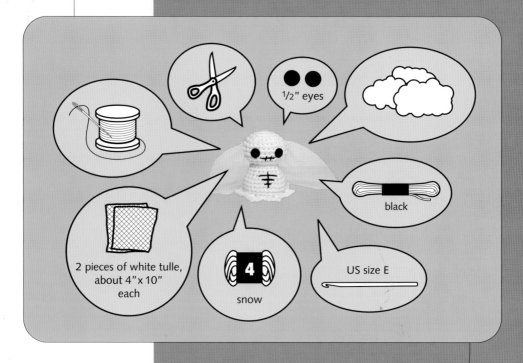

Basics

Head
Use snow-colored yarn and make 1 Basic Head (see pattern on page 95).

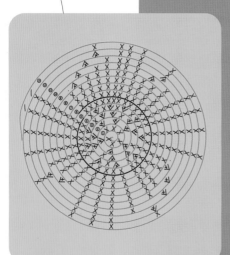

Body
Use snow-colored yarn.
Row 1: Sc 6 in magic ring† {6}.
Row 2: [Inc] around {12}.
Row 3: [Inc, inc, sc 1] around {20}.
Row 4: [Inc, sc 1] around {30}.
Row 5: Sc around {30}.
Row 6: Sc around in back loops {30}.
Row 7: Sc around {30}.
Row 8: Sc around {30}.
Row 9: [Sc 13, dec] around {28}.
Row 10: [Sc 5, dec] around {24}.
Row 11: [Sc 4, dec] around {20}.
Row 12: [Sc 8, dec] around {18}.
Row 13: Sc around, sl st, sl st. Clean fasten off† {18}.
Join again in the front loops left from row 6.

† Stitches explained on pages 12 and 14.

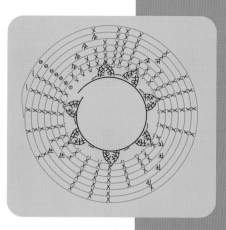

Work around: [Skip 1, dc 3 in 1, ch 1, sl st in front 2 loops of prev dc, dc 3 in same space as prev. dc 3, skip 1, sl st] around. Clean fasten off†.

† Stitch explained on page 14.

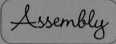
Assembly

1. Stuff head and body and stitch together.

2. Using black embroidery floss, stitch rib cage.

3. Using black embroidery floss, stitch mouth.

4. Attach eyes.

5. Gather both pieces of veil and tack around head. They should be gathered enough to fit around about half of the head.

Basics

Head and Body
Use snow-colored yarn and make 1 Basic Head. Use charcoal-colored yarn and make 1 Basic Body. (See patterns on pages 94–95.)

Details

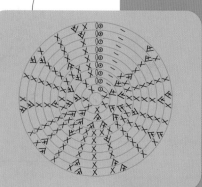

Hat
Use charcoal-colored yarn.
Row 1: Sc 6 in magic ring†, sl st to close round {6}.
Row 2: Ch 1, sc 1 in same, [inc] around, sl st to close round {11}.
Row 3: Ch 1, sc 1 in same, [inc] around, sl st to close round {23}.
Row 4: Ch 1, sc around in back loops, sl st to close {23}.
Row 5: Ch 1, sc 1, dec, [sc 2, dec] around, sl st to close round.

† Stitch explained on page 12.

Row 6: Ch 1, sc around, sl st to close round {17}.
Row 7: Ch 1, sc around, sl st to close round {17}.
Row 8: Ch 1, working in front loops: inc, [sc 1, inc] around, sl st to close round {26}.
Row 9: Ch 1, sc 1, inc, [sc 2, inc] around, sl st to close {35}. Fasten off.

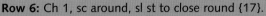

Assembly

1. Stuff head and body and stitch together.

2. Using white embroidery floss, stitch rib cage.

3. Using black embroidery floss, stitch mouth.

4. Attach eyes.

5. Stitch on hat, placed at a jaunty angle.

MEDUSA

Bad hair day. Seriously.

Difficulty Level: Intermediate • **Gauge:** 5 sc x 5 rows = 1" x 1"

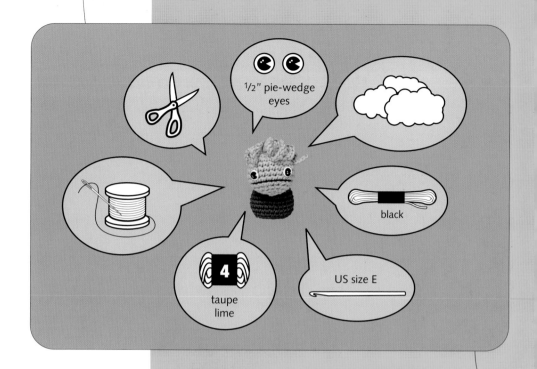

Basics

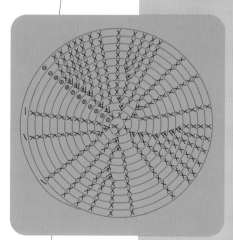

Body

Use taupe-colored yarn.

Row 1: Sc 6 in magic ring† {6}.
Row 2: [Inc] around {12}.
Row 3: [Sc 1, inc] around {18}.
Row 4: Sc around {18}.
Row 5: [Sc 8, inc] twice {20}.
Row 6: [Sc 4, inc] around {24}.
Row 7: [Sc 5, inc] around {28}.
Row 8: [Sc 13. inc] around {30}.
Row 9: Sc around {30}.
Row 10: Sc around {30}.
Row 11: Sc around {30}.
Row 12: Sc around, sl st, sl st {30}.
Clean fasten off†.

Base

Use taupe-colored yarn.

Row 1: Sc 6 in magic ring†, sl st to close round {6}.
Row 2: Ch 1, sc 1 in same, [inc] around, sl st to close round {11}.

† Stitches explained on pages 12 and 14.

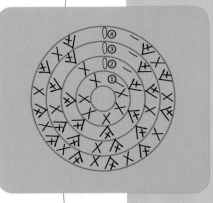

Row 3: Ch 1, inc, inc, [sc 1, inc, inc] around, sl st to close round {19}.
Row 4: Before working each stitch in this round, put the hook through the back loop of the next st on the edge of the top piece, thus joining the top and base. (Alternately, you may work the round normally and stitch together the top and base afterward.) Ch 1, inc, [sc 1, inc] around {29}. Clean fasten off†.

† Stitch explained on page 14.

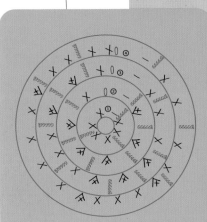

Head
Use lime-colored yarn.
{snake} = ch 6, sl st 5 back to beg of chain
Row 1: [Sc 2, {snake}] 3 times in magic ring†, sl st to close {6 sc}.
Row 2: Ch 1, sc 1 in same, {snake}, [sc 2 in 1, {snake}], sl st to close {11 sc}.
Row 3: Ch 1, sc in same, {snake}, [sc 2 in 1, {snake}] 2 times, sc 2, {snake}, sc 1, [sc 2 in 1, {snake}] 3 times, sc 2, {snake}, sc 1, sl st to close {17 sc}.
Row 4: [sc 2, {snake}] 2 times, sc 1, sc 2 in 1, sc 5, sc 2 in 1, [sc 2, {snake}] 2 times, sc 1, sc 2 in 1, {snake}, sl st to close {20 sc}.
Rows 5–12: Same as rows 5–12 of Basic Head pattern (see page 95).

† Stitch explained on page 12.

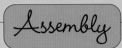

Assembly

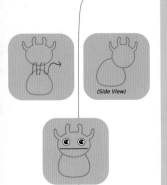

(Side View)

1. Stuff head and body and stitch head to front of body, as close to the top as possible. Medusa is a bit front-heavy because of the way her head is attached (see "side view"), so it helps to weight the bottom of her body with poly-pellets or heavy stuffing materials.

2. Using black embroidery floss, stitch mouth. Attach eyes.

FUZZY ALIEN

Loveable, in an otherworldly way.

Difficulty Level: Beginner • **Gauge:** 3 sc x 3 rows = 1" x 1"

Basics

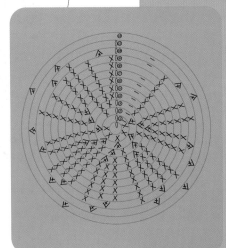

Body

Use one strand of terracotta and one strand of moulin rouge together.

Row 1: Ch 2, sc 5 in first ch st, sl st to close round {5}.

Row 2: Ch 1, sc 1 in same, [inc] 5 times, sl st to close round {11}.

Row 3: Ch 1, sc 1 in same, sc 1, [inc, sc 1] 5 times, sl st to close round {17}.

Row 4: Ch 1, sc 1 in same, sc 2, [inc, sc 2] 5 times, sl st to close round {23}.

Row 5: Ch 1, sc around, sl st to close round {23}.

Row 6: Ch 1, sc around, sl st to close round {23}.

Row 7: Ch 1, sc around, sl st to close round {23}.

Row 8: Ch 1, sc around, sl st to close round {23}.

Row 9: Ch 1, sc around, sl st to close round {23}.

Row 10: Ch 1, dec, [sc 1, dec] around, sl st to close round {15}.

Row 11: Ch 1, [dec] around.

Row 12: Dec to close. Fasten off and stitch closed.

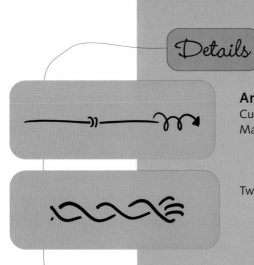

Details

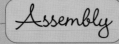

Antennae
Cut two 5"-long pieces of snow-colored yarn.
Make a knot in the center of each.

Twist and fold in half.

Assembly

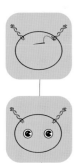

1. Pull loose ends of antennae through top of body and stitch in place.

2. Attach eyes.

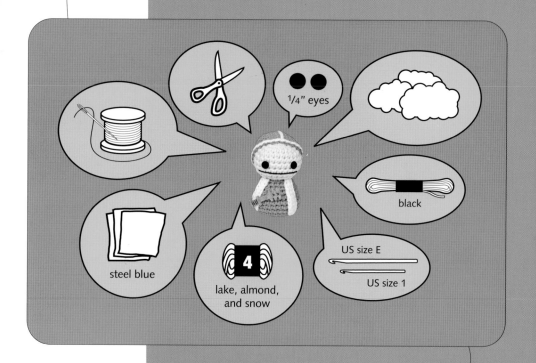

steel blue

lake, almond, and snow

US size E

US size 1

black

1/4" eyes

Basics

Head and Body

Use size E hook and almond-colored yarn and make 1 Basic Head. Use lake-colored yarn and make 1 Basic Body. (See patterns on pages 94–95.)

Details

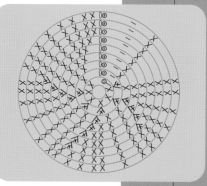

Cap

Use lake-colored yarn.

Row 1: Sc 6 in magic ring†. Sl st to close round {6}.

Row 2: Ch 1, sc 1 in same, [inc] around, sl st to close {11}.

Row 3: Ch 1, sc 1, inc, [sc 2, inc] around, sl st to close {15}.

Row 4: Ch 1, sc 2, inc, [sc 3, inc] around, sl st to close {19}.

Row 5: Ch 1, sc 3, inc, [sc 4, inc] around, sl st to close {23}.

† Stitch explained on page 12.

Row 6: Ch 1, sc 4, inc, [sc 5, inc] around, sl st to close {27}.
Row 7: Ch 1, sc 12, inc, [sc 13, inc] around, sl st to close {29}.
Row 8: Ch 1, sc around, sl st to close {29}.
Row 9: Same as row 8. Fasten off.
Switch to size 1 hook and snow-colored yarn. Make a straight stitch on the front, from the base to top of cap. Chain stitch around edge.

Stole
Use size E hook and snow-colored yarn and make 2. Ch 10, sl st 2 loops from hook, hdc 8. Fasten off.

Mace
Fashion a mace from felt (see "Arms & Armaments," page 18).

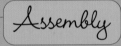

Assembly

1. Stuff head and body and stitch together.

2. Stitch cap onto head.

3. Using black embroidery floss, stitch mouth.

4. Stitch stole pieces onto body.

5. Stitch or glue the mace onto body. Attach eyes.

AMAZON

C'mon. Just give her a reason.

Difficulty Level: Intermediate • **Gauge:** 5 sc x 5 rows = 1" x 1"

3/8" eyes

black

almond taupe

US size E

Head and Body

Use almond-colored yarn and make 1 Basic Head and 1 Basic Body (see patterns on pages 94–95).

Details

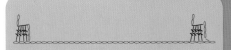

Bikini Top

Use taupe-colored yarn.

Row 1: Ch 36, sl st 2 loops from hook, ch 3, tr 2 in 1, leaving last 2 loops on hook, tr 2 in 1, pulling last loop through all loops on hook, ch 2. Fasten off.

Row 2: Join 3 sts from end of chain. Ch 3, tr 1 in same, leaving last 2 loops on hook, tr 2 in 1, tr 1, ch 2. Fasten off.

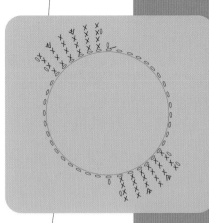

Bikini Bottom

Use taupe-colored yarn.

Row 1: Ch 40, sl st in first ch to make a ring.
Row 2: Ch 1, sc 6.
Row 3: Ch 1, flip, sc 6.
Row 4: Ch 1, flip, sc 6.
Row 5: Ch 1, flip, sc 1, sc 2 in 1, sc 1, sc 2 in 1, sc 2. Fasten off.
Row 6: Join 14 sts from end of row 2, ch 1, sc 6.
Row 7: Ch 1, flip, sc 6.
Row 8: Ch 1, flip, sc 6.
Row 9: Ch 1, flip, sc 1, sc 2 in 1, sc 1, sc 2 in 1, sc 2. Fasten off.

Spear

Craft a spear from clay (see "Arms & Armaments," page 18).

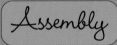

Assembly

1. Stuff head and body and stitch together.

2. Create hair and stitch onto head (see "Hair," page 15). Tie in a ponytail with a piece of matching yarn and pull a few strands down in front.

3. Stitch bikini onto body.

4. Using black embroidery floss, stitch mouth. Attach eyes.

5. Attach spear with glue.

CORPORATE ZOMBIE

Eat. Sleep. Work. Brains.

Difficulty Level: Intermediate • **Gauge:** 5 sc x 5 rows = 1" x 1"

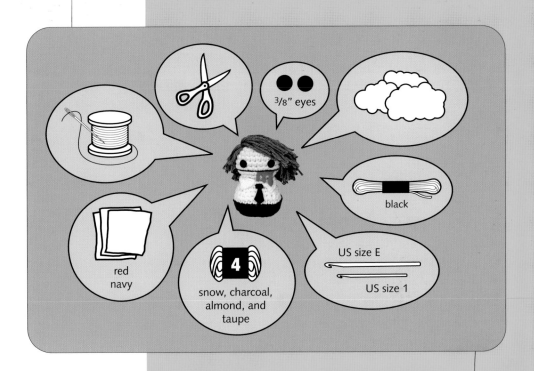

Basics

Head

Use size E hook and almond-colored yarn. Make 1 Basic Head (see pattern on page 95).

Body

Use size E hook and charcoal-colored yarn. Work rows 1–7 of Basic Body (see pattern on page 94).
Switch to snow-colored yarn and continue to end.
Switch to a size 1 hook and charcoal-colored yarn. Chain stitch around body between charcoal- and snow-colored sections.

Details

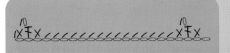

Work-Shirt Collar

Use size E hook and snow-colored yarn. Ch 22, sc 1, dc 1, ch 1, sl st in front 2 loops of prev dc, sc 1, sl st 15, sc 1, dc 1, ch 1, sl st in front 2 loops, sc 1, sl st in same. Fasten off.

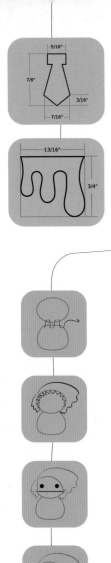

Tie
Cut navy felt according to template.

Dripping Blood
Cut red felt according to template.

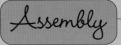

1. Stuff head and body and stitch together.

2. Make fringe hair (see directions on page 15). Stitch one piece of hair fringe in a zigzag along side of head. Stitch another piece of hair fringe in a zigzag along other side of head. Keep hair arranged with a part on the side and trim ends.

3. Using black embroidery, stitch mouth. Attach eyes.

4. Arrange collar around neck and stitch in place.

5. Stitch or glue blood into place under mouth. Do the same for the tie.

GRIM REAPER

Death has many faces. This one's pretty cute.

Difficulty Level: Beginner • **Gauge:** 5 sc x 5 rows = 1" x 1"

Basics

Head and Body

Use almond-colored yarn and make 1 Basic Head. Use charcoal-colored yarn and make 1 Basic Body. (See patterns on pages 94–95.)

Details

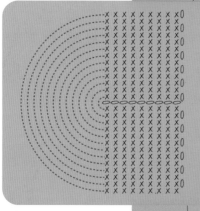

Hood

Use charcoal-colored yarn. Ch 10, sc 9 along chain, continue around to other side of chain, sc 9, [ch 1, flip, sc 18] 12 times. Fasten off.

Scythe

Craft a scythe from clay (see "Arms & Armaments," page 18).

Assembly

1. Stuff head and body and stitch together.

2. Stitch hood onto head.

3. Using black embroidery floss, stitch mouth. Attach eyes.

4. Attach scythe with glue.

TROJAN

Always there when you need him.

Difficulty Level: Epic • **Gauge:** 5 sc x 5 rows = 1" x 1"

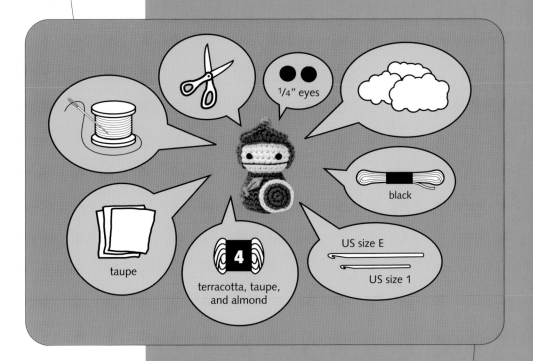

1/4" eyes

black

US size E

US size 1

terracotta, taupe,
and almond

taupe

Head and Body

Use size E hook and almond-colored yarn and make 1 Basic Head. Use taupe-colored yarn and make 1 Basic Body. (See patterns on pages 94–95.)

Details

Shield

Use size E hook and taupe-colored yarn.
Row 1: Sc 8 in magic ring†, sl st to close round {8}.
Row 2: Ch 1, sc 1 in same, inc around, sl st to close round {15}.
Row 3: Ch 1, sc 1 in same, sc 1, [inc, sc 1] around {23}.
Clean fasten off†.
Switch to size 1 hook and almond-colored yarn. Chain stitch around edge.

† Stitches explained on pages 12 and 14.

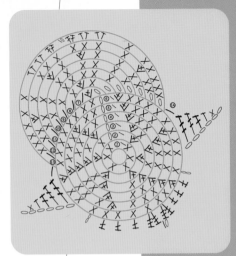

Helmet

Use size E hook and taupe-colored yarn.

Row 1: Sc 6 in magic ring†, sl st to close round {6}.

Row 2: Ch 1, sc 1 in same, [inc] around, sl st to close {11}.

Row 3: Ch 1, inc, [sc 1, inc] around, sl st to close {17}.

Row 4: Ch 1, sc 1, inc, [sc 2, inc] around, sl st to close {23}.

Row 5: Ch 1, sc 2, inc, [sc 3, inc] around, sl st to close {29}.

Row 6: Ch 1, sc 8, inc, [sc 9, inc] around, sl st to close {32}.

Row 7: Ch 1, inc, clean fasten off† {2}.

Row 8: Join before ch 1 of last row. ch 1, sc 1, inc, sc 1, clean fasten off† in next st {4}.

Row 9: Join before ch 1 of last row. ch 1, sc 6, clean fasten off† in next st {6}.

Row 10: Join before ch 1 of last row. ch 1, sc 8, clean fasten off† in next st {8}.

Row 11: Join before ch 1 of last row. ch 1, sc 4, inc, sc 1, inc, sc 3, clean fasten off† in next st {12}.

Row 12: Join before ch 1 of last row, ch 1, sc 2, inc, sc 8, inc, sc 2, clean fasten off† in next st {16}.

Row 13: Join before ch 1 of last row, ch 1, sc 6, [hdc 2 in 1] twice, dc 2 in 1, ch 1, sl st in front 2 loops of last dc, dc 2 in 1, [hdc 2 in 1] twice, sc 6. Clean fasten off† in next st {24}.

Row 14: Join 4 sts before ch of last row. Ch 6, working in the ch 6 just made, sc 1, hdc 1, dc 1, tr 2, sl st in the same space as the ch 1 of the last row {5}. Fasten off.

Repeat row 14 on opposite side of helmet (4 sts from the end of row 13), working stitches backward so that the "right side" of the stitch faces out. Alternately, you may join in the same stitch as the end of row 13 and repeat row 14, working the final st 4 sts away from the end of row 13.

To form the front of the helmet (working in the front/top loops), join in the next open st after row 14. Ch 2, dc 3, tr 2 in 1, ch 1, sl st in front 2 loops of last tr, tr 2 in 1, dc 3, ch 2. Pull this loop through the last open st of helmet front to fasten off.

† Stitches explained on pages 12 and 14.

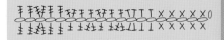

Crest

Use size E hook and terracotta-colored yarn.
Ch 20, sc 5, hdc 2, hdc 2 in 1, [dc 2, dc 2 in 1] twice, tr 2, tr 2 in 1, tr 2.

Continue around the end of ch, working on opposite side: Tr 2, tr 2 in 1, tr 2, [dc 2, dc 2 in 1] twice, hdc 2 in 1, hdc 2, sc 5. Fasten off.

Fold in half so that the stitches formed on one side of the ch are against the stitch formed on the other side. Sew the top edges of the two sides together.

Sword

Fashion a sword from felt (see "Arms & Armaments," page 18).

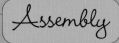

Assembly

1. Stuff head and body and stitch together.

2. Stitch helmet onto head. It may help to pin it in place before stitching to ensure even placement.

3. Stitch crest onto top of helmet.

4. Stitch shield onto front of body. Stitch or glue felt sword onto body, opposite shield.

5. Using black embroidery floss, stitch mouth. Attach eyes.

SPARTAN

He's rather terse. Laconic, even.

Difficulty Level: Epic • **Gauge:** 5 sc x 5 rows = 1" x 1"

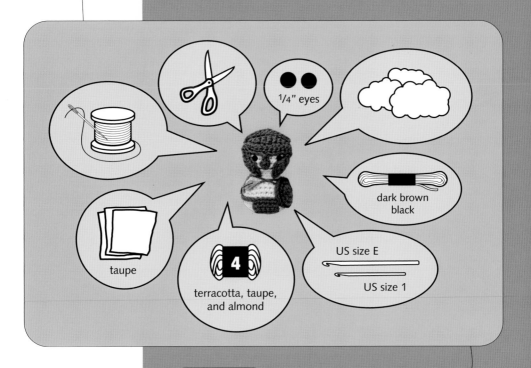

1/4" eyes

dark brown
black

taupe

4

terracotta, taupe,
and almond

US size E

US size 1

Head and Body
*Use size E hook and almond-colored yarn and make 1 Basic
Head and 1 Basic Body. (See patterns on pages 94–95.)*

Details

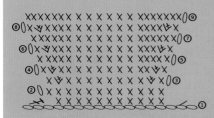

Cape
Use size E hook and terracotta-colored yarn.
Row 1: Ch 17, sl st, skip 1, sc 11, skip 2, dc 1.
Row 2: Ch 1, flip, sc 12 {12}.
Row 3: Ch 1, flip, sc 1, inc, sc 8, inc, sc 1 {14}.
Row 4: Ch 1, flip, sc 1, inc, sc 10, inc, sc 1 {16}.
Row 5: Ch 1, flip, sc 16 {16}.
Row 6: Ch 1, flip, sc 1, inc, sc 12, inc, sc 1 {18}.
Row 7: Ch 1, flip, sc 18 {18}.
Row 8: Ch 1, flip, sc 1, inc, sc 14, inc, sc 1 {20}.
Row 9: Ch 1, flip, sc 20, fasten off {20}.

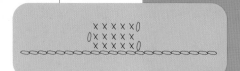

Loin Cloth

Use size E hook and taupe-colored yarn. Ch 22, cut. join 9 sts from beginning, ch 1, sc 5, ch 1, flip, sc 5, ch 1, flip, sc 5. Fasten off.

Shield

Use size E hook and taupe-colored yarn.
Row 1: Sc 8 in magic ring[†], sl st to close round {8}.
Row 2: Ch 1, sc 1 in same, inc around, sl st to close round {15}.
Row 3: Ch 1, sc 1 in same, sc 1, [inc, sc 1] around {23}.
Clean fasten off[†].
Switch to size 1 hook and dark brown embroidery floss.
Chain stitch around edge.

Helmet

Use size E hook and taupe-colored yarn.
Row 1: Sc 6 in magic ring[†], sl st to close round {6}.
Row 2: Ch 1, sc 1 in same, inc around, sl st to close round {11}.
Row 3: Ch 1, sc 1 in same, sc 1, [inc, sc 1] around, sl st to close round {17}.
Row 4: Ch 1, sc 1 in same, sc 2, [inc, sc 2] around, sl st to close round {23}.
Row 5: Ch 1, sc 1 in same, sc 7, [inc, sc 7] around, sl st to close round {26}.
Row 6: Ch 1, sc 1 in same, sc 8, [inc, sc 8] around, sl st to close round {29}.
Row 7: Ch 1, sc 1 in same, sc 9, [inc, sc 9] around {32}. Clean fasten off[†].

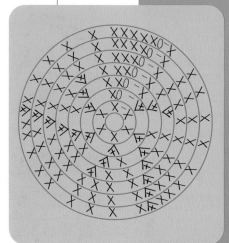

Row 8: Join again in clean fasten off. Working only in front loops, with right side of stitches facing out, ch 1, sc 2, hdc 2, [dc 1, ch 1, sl st in front 2 loops of prev dc, dc 1] in 1, hdc 2, sc 2, ch 1. Cut yarn and pull through next open st.

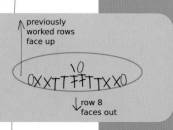

previously worked rows face up

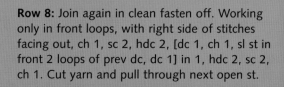

↓row 8
faces out

Row 9: Join again in the same place where the yarn was pulled through, this time working in the back loops, with the right sides of the stitches facing out: Hdc 1, dc 1, tr 2, dtr 1, tr 2, dc 1, hdc 1. Cut yarn and pull through the next open stitch.

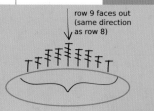

row 9 faces out
(same direction as row 8)

[†] Stitches explained on pages 12 and 14.

Row 10: Join in same space as in prev row. Sc 1, dc 2, dc 2 in 1, dc 1, ch 4, sl st, ch 1, sl st in same space as prev sl st, ch 1, sl st in same space as prev sl st, sl st, sl st, dc 1, dc 2 in 1, dc 2, sc 1. Cut yarn and pull through same space as prev yarn.

Row 11: Join in space before join from prev row. sc 1, dc 1, ch 7, sl st, ch 3, tr 1 in 2, dc 1 in 2, dc 1. Clean fasten off† in space after first dc.

† Stitch explained on page 14.

Row 12: Join 2 spaces from where yarn was pulled through last, ch 7, sl st, tr 2 in 1, dc 2 in 1, sc 2 in 1, dc 1 , sc 1. Cut yarn and pull through space after last yarn was pulled through.

Sword
Fashion a sword from felt (see "Arms & Armaments," page 18).

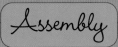

Assembly

1. Stuff head and body and stitch together.

2. Stitch helmet onto head and over face. It may help to pin it in place before stitching to ensure even placement.

3. Attach eyes between the gaps in helmet. Using black embroidery floss, stitch mouth.

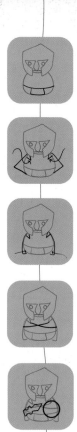

4. Stitch loincloth across front of body, about 6 rows down from where body meets head.

5. Pull upper corners of cape around shoulders and tack in place. The cape bottom should flare out slightly.

6. Tack bottom corners of cape to lower body. Then tack the rest of lower edge of cape to body at evenly spaced intervals to create a bit of a wave along lower edge.

7. With a length of taupe-colored yarn, crisscross the chest, connecting the two upper points of the cape. Tack in place.

8. Attach shield onto one side of body and felt sword onto the other.

CYBER ZOMBIE

Just needs to recharge—with some brains!

Difficulty Level: Epic • **Gauge:** 5 sc x 5 rows = 1" x 1"

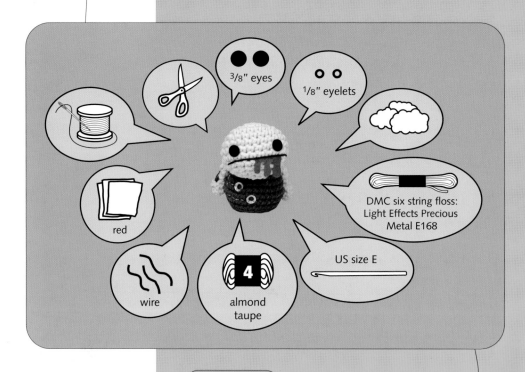

Head

Use almond-colored yarn and make 1 Basic Head (see pattern on page 95).

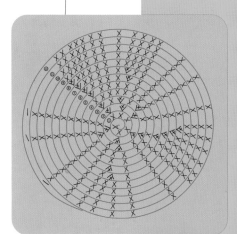

Body

Use taupe-colored yarn.
Row 1: Sc 6 in magic ring† {6}.
Row 2: [Inc] around {12}.
Row 3: [Sc 1, inc] around {18}.
Row 4: Sc around {18}.
Row 5: [Sc 8, inc] twice {20}.
Row 6: [Sc 4, inc] around {24}.
Row 7: [Sc 5, inc] around {28}.
Row 8: [Sc 13, inc] around {30}.
Row 9: Sc around {30}.
Row 10: Sc around {30}.
Row 11: Sc around {30}.
Row 12: Sc around, sl st, sl st {30}. Clean fasten off†.

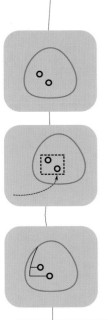

Before working the base of body, set eyelets along the front, as shown.

Attach a section of red felt behind each eyelet so that the color shows through the holes.

Using silver embroidery floss, stitch on wires.

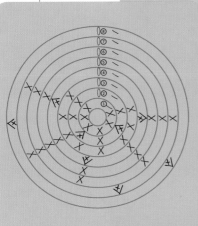

Base

Continue using taupe-colored yarn and work the rest of the body as follows:

Row 1: Sc 6 in magic ring†, sl st to close round {6}.

Row 2: Ch 1, sc 1 in same, [inc] around, sl st to close round {11}.

Row 3: Ch 1, inc, inc, [sc 1, inc, inc] around, sl st to close round {19}.

Row 4: Before working each stitch in this round, put the hook through the back loop of the next st on the edge of the top piece, thus joining the top and base. (Alternately, you may work the round normally and stitch together the top and base afterward.) Ch 1, inc, [sc 1, inc] around {29}. Clean fasten off†.

Arms

Use almond-colored yarn and make 2 arms.

Row 1: Sc 6 in magic ring†, sl st to close round {6}.

Row 2: Ch 1, sc 1 in same, sc 1, [sc 2 in 1, sc 1] around, sl st to close round {9}.

Row 3: Ch 1, sc around, sl st to close round {9}.

Row 4: Ch 1, dec, [sc 1, dec] around, sl st to close round {6}.

Row 5: Ch 1, sc around, sl st to close round {6}.

† Stitches explained on pages 12 and 14.

Row 6: Ch 1, sc around, sl st to close round {6}.
Row 7: Ch 1, sc 2, dec, sc 1, sl st to close round {5}.
Row 8: Ch 1, dec, dec, sl st. Fasten off. (Note that it helps to work in just the front loops for this row.)

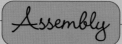

Assembly

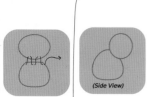

(Side View)

1. Stuff head and body and stitch together onto front of body, as close to the top as possible. Cyber zombie is a bit front-heavy because of the way his head is attached (see "side view"), so it helps to weight the base with poly-pellets or hefty stuffing material.

2. Attach arms to either side of body.

3. Cut open one arm to make room for the wires. (This is going to look messy and unraveled—it's supposed to! He'll survive.) Cut a few segments of wire, each a bit longer than the gash in the arm. (I used bits of wire from an old telephone cable.) Push the wire segments into the arm so that the ends are hidden inside. Use Fray Check to stanch the "wound."

4. Using black embroidery floss, stitch mouth. Attach eyes.

KNIGHT

He follows in a long tradition of legless, armless knights.

Difficulty Level: Intermediate • **Gauge:** 5 sc x 5 rows = 1" x 1"

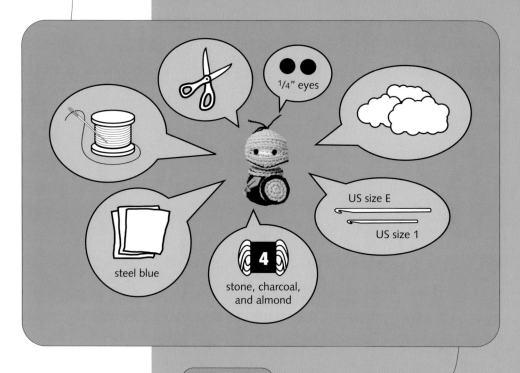

steel blue

stone, charcoal, and almond

¹/₄" eyes

US size E

US size 1

Basics

Head and Body
Use size E hook and almond-colored yarn and make 1 Basic Head. Use charcoal-colored yarn and make 1 Basic Body. (See patterns on pages 94–95.)

Details

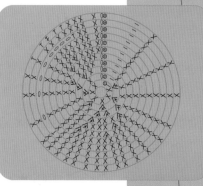

Helmet
Use size E hook and stone-colored yarn.
Row 1: Sc 6 in magic ring†, sl st to close round {6}.
Row 2: Ch 1, sc 1 in same, [inc] around, sl st to close round {11}.
Row 3: Ch 1, sc 1 in same, inc, inc, sc 3, [inc] 3 times, sc 3, sl st to close round {17}.
Row 4: Ch 1, sc 1 in same, sc 3, inc, sc 4, inc, sc 3, inc, sc 4, sl st to close round {21}.
Row 5: Ch 1, sc 1 in same, sc 3, inc, sc 6, inc, sc 3, inc, sc 6, sl st to close round {25}.

† Stitch explained on page 12.

Row 6: Ch 1, sc 1 in same, sc 3, inc, sc 8, inc, sc 3, inc, sc 8, sl st to close round {29}.
Row 7: Ch 1, sc around in back loops, sl st to close round.
Row 8: Ch 1, sc around, sl st to close round {29}.
Row 9: Ch 1, sc 3, hdc 1, ch 8, skip 8, hdc 1, sc around, sl st to close round {29}.
Row 10: Ch 1, sc around, sl st to close round {29}.
Row 11: Ch 1, sc 4, hdc 2, dc 1, hdc 2, sc around {29}. Clean fasten off[†].
Switch to size 1 hook and charcoal-colored yarn. Chain stitch around wrong side of lower edge.

[†] Stitch explained on page 14.

Tassel
Cut two 5" sections of charcoal yarn.
Hold the two pieces together and make a knot in the middle. Fold in half. Pull loose ends through top of helmet and stitch in place. Trim ends.

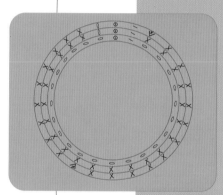

Collar
Use size E hook and stone-colored yarn.
Row 1: Ch 23, sl st to close round.
Row 2: Ch 1, sc around, sl st to close round.
Row 3: Ch 1, sc 9, inc, sc 11, inc, clean fasten off[†].
Switch to size 1 hook and charcoal-colored yarn. Chain stitch around wrong side of lower edge.

Shield
Use size E hook and stone-colored yarn.
Row 1: Sc 8 in magic ring[†], sl st to close round {8}.
Row 2: Ch 1, sc 1 in same, inc around, sl st to close round {15}.
Row 3: Ch 1, sc 1 in same, sc 1, [inc, sc 1] around {23}. Clean fasten off[†].
Switch to size 1 hook and charcoal-colored yarn. Chain stitch around edge.

[†] Stitches explained on pages 12 and 14.

Sword
Fashion a sword from felt (see "Arms & Armaments," page 18).

Assembly

1. Stuff body. Nest body in collar and stitch in place.

2. Stuff head and stitch to body.

3. Stitch helmet onto head and over face.

4. Stitch shield onto front of body.

5. Stitch or glue sword onto other side of body.

6. Attach eyes.

NINJA

Tiny. Stealthy. Deadly. Cute.

Difficulty Level: Beginner • **Gauge:** 5 sc x 5 rows = 1" x 1"

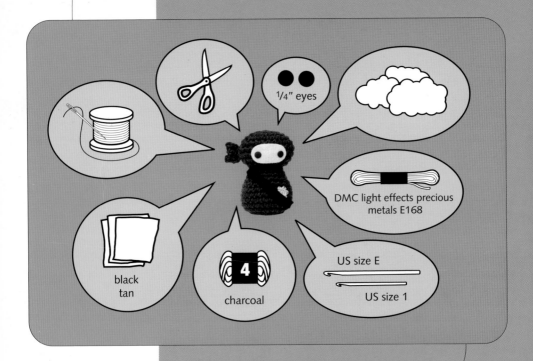

Basics

Head and Body
Use size E hook and charcoal-colored yarn. Make 1 Basic Head and 1 Basic Body. (See patterns on pages 94–95.)

Details

Tie
Use size E hook and charcoal-colored yarn. [Ch 3, dc 1 in first ch st, ch 1, sl st in front two loops of prev dc, ch 3, sl st in same st as prev dc] twice. Fasten off.

Ninja Star
Use size 1 hook and embroidery floss. [Ch 1, {sc 1, ch 2, sl st in front two loops of prev sc} 6 times] in magic ring[†]. Fasten off.

† Stitch explained on page 12.

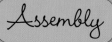

1. Stuff head and body and stitch together.

2. Stitch tie to side of head.

3. Stitch ninja star to front of body.

4. Cut a strip of black felt, about 1/4" wide and 7" long. Loop around body and stitch or glue in place.

5. Cut a rounded rectangle of tan-colored felt, about 1 1/2" wide and 3/4" tall. Stitch or glue to head.

6. Attach eyes.

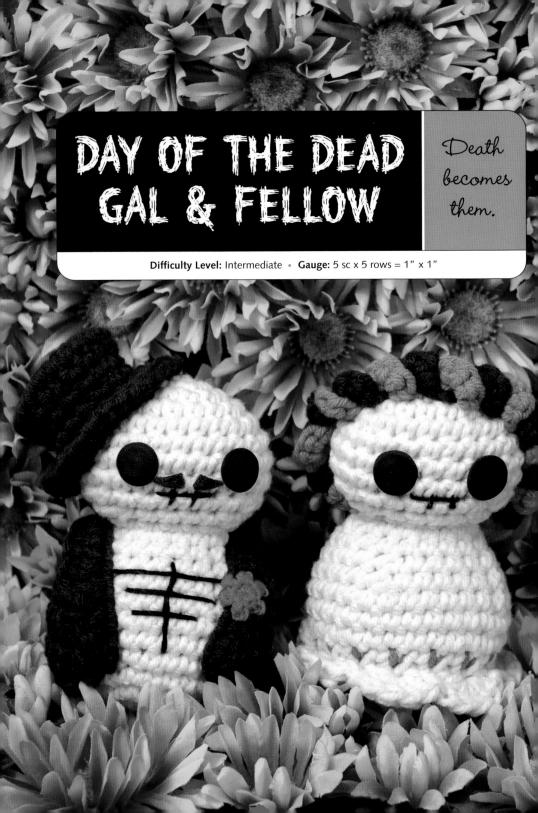

DAY OF THE DEAD GAL & FELLOW

Death becomes them.

Difficulty Level: Intermediate • **Gauge:** 5 sc x 5 rows = 1" x 1"

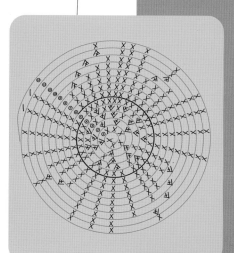

Basics

Head

Use almond-colored yarn and make 1 Basic Head (see pattern on page 95).

Body

Use almond-colored yarn.

Row 1: Sc 6 in magic ring† {6}.

Row 2: [inc] around {12}.

Row 3: [inc, inc, sc 1] around {20}.

Row 4: [inc, sc 1] around {30}.

Row 5: Sc around {30}.

Row 6: Sc around in back loops in pattern stitch†, using almond- and terracotta-colored yarns {30}.

Row 7: Sc around {30}.

Row 8: Sc around {30}.

Row 9: [Sc 13, dec] around {28}.

Row 10: [Sc 5, dec] around {24}.

Row 11: [Sc 4, dec] around {20}.

Row 12: [Sc 8, dec] around {18}.

† Stitches explained on pages 12–13.

Row 13: Sc around, sl st, sl st {18}. Clean fasten off[†].
Join again in the front loops left from row 6. Work as follows:
[Skip 1, dc 5 in 1, skip 1, sl st] around. Clean fasten off[†].

† Stitch explained on page 14.

Crown
Make one in terracotta-colored yarn and one in charcoal-colored yarn. [Ch 4, sc 3 in 1, sl st in same] 12 times. Fasten off.

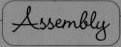

Assembly

1. Stuff head and body and stitch together.

2. Using black embroidery floss, stitch mouth.

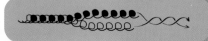

3. Twist the two differently colored pieces of the crown around each other.

4. Coil the spiral around the head, like a wreath, and stitch in place, with the join at the back of head.

5. Attach eyes.

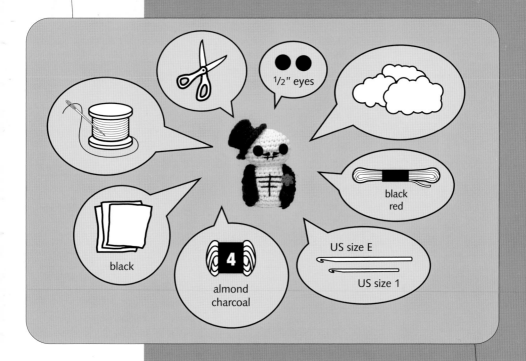

Basics

Head and Body

Use size E hook and almond-colored yarn. Make 1 Basic Head and 1 Basic Body. (See patterns on pages 94–95.)

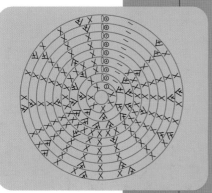

Hat

Use size E hook and charcoal-colored yarn.

Row 1: Sc 6 in magic ring†, sl st to close round {6}.

Row 2: Ch 1, sc 1 in same, [inc] around, sl st to close round {11}.

Row 3: Ch 1, sc 1 in same, [inc] around, sl st to close round {23}.

Row 4: Ch 1, sc around in back loops, sl st to close {23}.

Row 5: Ch 1, sc 1, dec, [sc 2, dec] around, sl st to close round {17}.

† Stitch explained on page 12.

Row 6: Ch 1, sc around, sl st to close round {17}.
Row 7: Ch 1, sc around, sl st to close round {17}.
Row 8: Ch 1, working in front loops: inc, [sc 1, inc] around, sl st to close round {26}.
Row 9: Ch 1, sc 1, inc, [sc 2, inc] around, sl st to close {35}. Fasten off.

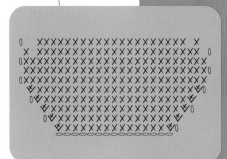

Vest

Use size E hook and charcoal-colored yarn.
Row 1: Ch 16.
Row 2: Inc, sc 13, sc 2 in 1.
Row 3: Ch 1, flip, inc, sc 15, inc.
Row 4: Ch 1, flip, inc, sc 17, inc.
Row 5: Ch 1, flip, inc, sc 19, inc.
Row 6: Ch 1, flip, inc, sc 21, inc.
Row 7: Ch 1, flip, sc across.
Row 8: Ch 1, flip, sc across.
Row 9: Ch 1, flip, sc across.
Row 10: Ch 1, skip 1 sc 22, skip 1, sc 1.
Row 11: Ch 1, skip 1, sc 20, skip 1, sc 1. Fasten off.

Lapel

Use size E hook and charcoal-colored yarn. Ch 35, sc 1, hdc 1, dc 1, ch 1, sl st in front two loops of dc, sl st, ch 1, tr 1, dc 23, tr 1, ch 1, sl st in main chain, ch 2, sl st in ch 2, dc 1, hdc 1, sc 1. Clean fasten off[†].

Boutonniere

Use size 1 hook and red embroidery floss. Ch 1, [sc 1, ch 2, sl st in front two loops of prev. sc] 6 times in magic ring[†]. Fasten off.

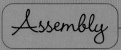

[†] Stitches explained on pages 12 and 14.

Assembly

1. Stuff head and body and stitch together.

2. Using black embroidery floss, stitch rib cage.

3. Using black embroidery floss, stitch mouth.

4. Attach eyes.

5. Cut 2 long, thin triangles of black felt (about 1/4" long and 1/8" wide) and glue directly above mouth.

6. Stuff hat lightly and stitch to head at a jaunty angle.

7. Wrap vest around body, about one row from where body meets head, and stitch in place.

8. Wrap lapel around neck, just above vest, and stitch in place.

9. Stitch boutonniere into place.

MONKEY

Everyone likes monkeys!

Difficulty Level: Epic • **Gauge:** 5 sc x 5 rows = 1" x 1"

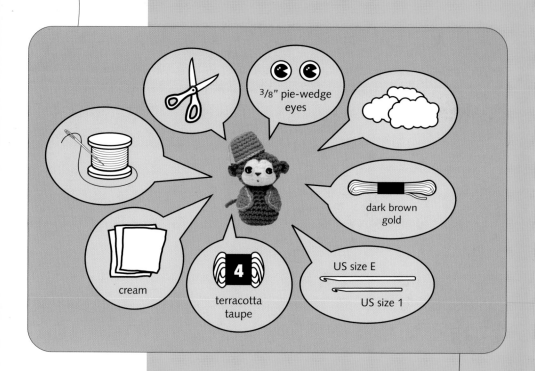

3/8" pie-wedge eyes

dark brown
gold

US size E
US size 1

cream

terracotta
taupe

Basics

Head and Body
Use size E hook and taupe-colored yarn. Make 1 Basic Head and 1 Basic Body. (See patterns on pages 94–95.)

Details

Ears
Use size E hook and taupe-colored yarn. Make one pair.
(Ch 2, dc 5) in magic ring†. Fasten off.

Tail
Use taupe-colored yarn. Ch 27, sl st 25.

Fez
Use size E hook and terracotta-colored yarn.
Row 1: Sc 6 in magic ring†, sl st to close {6}.
Row 2: Ch 1, sc 1 in same, inc around, sl st to close round {11}.
Row 3: Ch 1, sc 1 in same, sc 1, [inc, sc 1] around, sl st to close round {17}.

† Stitch explained on page 12.

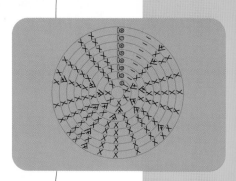

Row 4: Ch 1, working in back loops, sc around, sl st to close round {17}.
Row 5: Ch 1, sc around, sl st to close round {17}.
Row 6: Ch 1, sc 7, inc, sc 8, inc, sl st {19}.
Row 7: Ch 1, sc 3, inc, sc 9, inc, sc 5 {21}.
Row 8: Ch 1, sc 9, inc, sc 10, inc {23}. Clean fasten off[†].
Switch to size 1 hook and gold embroidery floss. Chain stitch around edge.

† Stitch explained on page 14.

Tassel

1. Cut 4 5"-long sections of gold embroidery floss. Fold 3 of them in half over the fourth.

2. Pull a single thread of the same floss, fold it in half over the same point, and thread the ends into a needle.

3. Wrap the thread around the bundle of floss a few times and stitch in place.

4. Twist the single 5" segment and fold in half, allowing it to twist. Pull the end through the top of the fez and stitch in place. Trim ends.

Vest

Use size E hook and terracotta-colored yarn.
Row 1: Ch 16.
Row 2: Inc, sc 13, inc {17}.
Row 3: Ch 1, flip, inc, sc 15, inc {19}.
Row 4: Ch 1, flip, inc, sc 17, inc {21}.
Row 5: Ch 1, flip, inc, sc 19, inc {23}.
Row 6: Ch 1, flip, sc across {23}.
Row 7: Ch 1, skip 1 sc 20, skip 1, sc 1 {21}.
Row 8: Ch 1, skip 1, sc 18, skip 1, sc 1, fasten off {19}.
Switch to size 1 hook and gold embroidery floss. Chain stitch around edge.

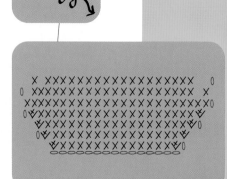

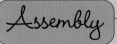

Assembly

1. Stuff head and body and stitch together.

2. Cut cream-colored felt according to template. Your template should be about 1 5/8" wide and 1 5/16" tall.

3. Stitch nose with padded satin stitch. Stitch mouth as a French knot.

4. Stitch or glue felt face to head. Attach eyes.

5. Stitch ears to either side of head.

6. Stuff fez lightly and stitch to head.

7. Wrap vest snugly around body and stitch in place.

8. Stitch tail to back of body.

ROBOT

Noop!

Difficulty Level: Intermediate • **Gauge:** 5 sc x 5 rows = 1" x 1"

Basics

Head and Body
Use size E hook and lake-colored yarn. Make 1 Basic Body and 1 Basic Head. (See patterns on pages 94–95.)

Details

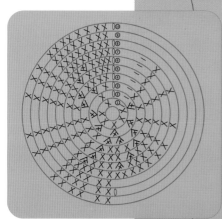

Helmet
Use size E hook and snow-colored yarn.
Row 1: Sc 6 in magic ring⁺, sl st to close round {6}.
Row 2: Ch 1, sc 1 in same, [inc] around, sl st to close round {11}.
Row 3: Ch 1, sc 1 in same, inc, inc, sc 3, [inc] 3 times, sc 3, sl st to close round {17}.
Row 4: Ch 1, sc 1 in same, sc 3, inc, sc 4, inc, sc 3, inc, sc 4, sl st to close round {21}.
Row 5: Ch 1, sc 1 in same, sc 3, inc, sc 6, inc, sc 3, inc, sc 6, sl st to close round {25}.
Row 6: Ch 1, sc 1 in same, sc 3, inc, sc 8, inc, sc 3, inc, sc 8, sl st to close round {29}.

Row 7: Ch 1, sc around, sl st to close round {29}.
Row 8: Ch 1, sc 19 {19}.
Row 9: Ch 1, flip, sc 19 {19}.
Row 10: Ch 1, flip, sc 19. Fasten off {19}.
Switch to size 1 hook and lake-colored yarn. Chain stitch around edge on wrong side (that is, flip the finished piece inside out and chain stitch as usual around the edge, then flip it right side out again).

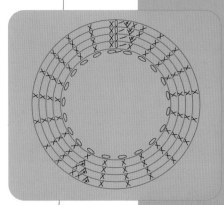

Shoulders

Use size E hook and snow-colored yarn.
Row 1: Ch 21, sl st in first ch st to make round.
Row 2: Ch 1, sc around, sl st to make round {21}.
Row 3: Ch 1, sc 9, inc, sc 10, inc, sl st to close round {23}.
Row 4: Ch 1, sc 10, inc, sc 11, inc, sl st to close round {25}.
Row 5: Ch 1, sc 11, inc, sc 13 {26}. Clean fasten off†.
Switch to size 1 hook and lake-colored yarn. Chain stitch around edge on wrong side.

Knobs

Use size E hook and lake-colored yarn. Make one pair. [Ch 2, hdc 7] in magic ring†. Clean fasten off†.

† Stitches explained on pages 12 and 14.

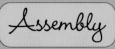

Assembly

1. Stuff body. Nest top of body inside shoulders and stitch in place.

2. Stuff head and stitch to body.

3. Arrange helmet on head and stitch in place.

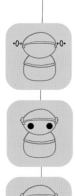

4. Stitch a knob to either side of helmet. Using snow-colored yarn, stitch a French knot through the center of each knob.

5. Attach eyes.

6. Using snow-colored yarn, stitch a single straight line between eyes.

BASIC BODY PARTS

This section contains instructions and diagrams to create all the common pattern pieces for the creatures: their bodies, arms, and heads. Mark this page—you'll refer to it again and again!

Basic Body

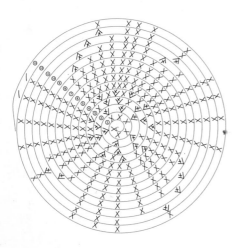

Row 1: Sc 6 in magic ring[†] {6}.
Row 2: [Inc] around {12}.
Row 3: [Inc, inc, sc 1] around {20}.
Row 4: [Inc, sc 1] around {30}.
Row 5: Sc around {30}.
Row 6: Sc around {30}.
Row 7: Sc around {30}.
Row 8: Sc around {30}.
Row 9: [Sc 13, dec] around {28}.
Row 10: [Sc 5, dec] around {24}.
Row 11: [Sc 4, dec] around {20}.
Row 12: [Sc 8, dec] around {18}.
Row 13: Sc around, sl st, sl st {18}. Clean fasten off[†].

Basic Arm

Row 1: Sc 6 in magic ring[†], sl st to close round.
Row 2: Ch 1, sc 1 in same, sc 1, [inc, sc 1] around, sl st to close round.
Row 3: Ch 1, sc around, clean fasten off[†].

[†] Stitches explained on pages 12 and 14.

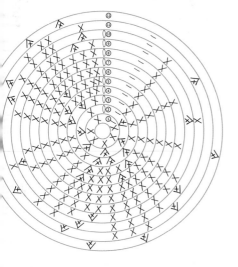

Row 1: Sc 6 in magic ring[†], sl st to close round {6}.

Row 2: Ch 1, sc 1 in same, [inc] around, sl st to close round {11}.

Row 3: Ch 1, sc 1 in same, inc, inc, sc 3, [inc] 3 times, sc 3, sl st to close round {17}.

Row 4: Ch 1, sc 1 in same, sc 3, inc, sc 4, inc, sc 3, inc, sc 4, sl st to close round {21}.

Row 5: Ch 1, sc 1 in same, sc 3, inc, sc 6, inc, sc 3, inc, sc 6, sl st to close round {25}.

Row 6: Ch 1, sc around, sl st to close round {25}.

Row 7: Ch 1, sc around, sl st to close round {25}.

Row 8: Ch 1, sc around, sl st to close round {25}.

Row 9: Ch 1, sc 1, dec, sc 6, dec, sc 3, dec, sc 6, dec, sc 1, sl st to close round {21}.

Row 10: Ch 1, dec, sc 4, dec, sc 3, dec, sc 4, dec, sc 2, sl st to close round {17}.

Row 11: Sc 4, [dec] 3 times, sc 3, [dec] twice, sl st to close round {12}.

Row 12: [Dec] around to close {6}. Fasten off and stitch base closed.

† Stitch explained on page 12.

CONVERSION CHART

A Note About Crochet Hooks: Hooks are available in plastic, steel, wood, and many other materials. They all feature the same parts—point, throat, shaft, thumb rest, and handle—and are sized according to the shaft's thickness. Because the lettering and numbers of hooks may vary, and the U.K. numbering system is the opposite of the U.S. system, it is best to look for the size in millimeters, which is always indicated on the hook.

All the projects in this book can be made using a U.S. size E hook, with finer details calling for a U.S. size 1. Below are these hooks' metric conversions.

Crochet Hook Sizes	
U.S.	**Metric (mm)**
B/1	2.25
E/4	3.5

Length	
Inches	**Centimeters**
1/8	0.3
3/16	0.5
1/4	0.65
3/8	1
1/2	1.25
3/4	2
1	2.5
11/2	4
2	5
3	7.5
4	10
5	12.5
6	15
7	17.5
8	20.5
9	23
10	25.5